*An
adoption
memoir*

Unselfish
LOVE

A. Smith

Copyright

I have tried to recreate events, locales and conversations from my memories of them. In order to maintain their anonymity in some instances I have changed the names of individuals and places, I may have changed some identifying characteristics and details such as physical properties, occupations and places of residence.

Printed in the United States of America

First Printing, 2019

Akennedy4313@gmail.com

For Sydney, who will always

hold a piece of my heart

Dumb and Dumber

June 2015

Sitting in the second row from the front of the altar at church, I listened as our preacher stood and talked about how the new six-week series was going to be called "Dumb and Dumber." Our guest speakers were, of course, Larry and Harry. The series discussed how people in the Bible did dumb things and then even dumber things to cover them up.

To be more precise, King David's dumb mistake was sleeping with another man's wife. What was even dumber, was that he ended up having the innocent man killed to cover up his own wrongdoing. Even though David's mistake was very dumb, God's love didn't budge. God continued to bless David once he endured his punishment for his dumb mistake.

King David is just one Bible hero. The Bible speaks of many more who did stupid things and then turned around and did idiotic things to cover them up. They tried to cover up things from the great I Am.

God knows we are sinful and that our second nature is to do reprehensible things to cover up our mistakes. While sitting in my seat, I realized that God loved me despite the dumb things I've done. My dumbest, yet greatest, feat began when I was 14 years old.

The Precious Life

February 16, 2001

She was beautiful. Her face was so smooth and perfect in every way. Every time I ran my finger over her cheek, I smiled as her lips twitched into a small smile. Her blue eyes seemed to hypnotize me. We could look into each other's eyes for hours. She weighed slightly more than a typical bag of sugar, and she fit into my arms as if she were the final puzzle piece. She made me feel complete.

"You need to eat," my dad told me.

"I know, but I'm not hungry," I answered.

Eating would take away my time with this precious little human who was in my stomach a few hours ago. I was only supposed to have two days with her. Thanks to an emergency C-section, I would spend four days with her.

After our time in the hospital, I didn't know when I would see her again. I knew I would have to wait until she turned 18 before I even had a chance. That was if she wanted to find me when she became of age.

"I made you," I said to the little bundle. "And you're beautiful."

I was awestruck—this baby, so tiny, had my heart. I put my finger in her hand and she squeezed. I laughed.

"Do you want to hold her?" I asked my dad.

Reluctantly, he agreed. He took her from my arms and sat next to the window. He smiled down at the little baby girl who was his biological granddaughter. I watched as his smile turned to a frown and he got up.

He placed the baby in my arms and began to cry.

Looking at my dad, I was confused with how his emotions could change so quickly. "What's wrong?"

He shook his head. "We can't keep her," he said choking on his words.

I nodded and tried not to cry. I looked down at the baby that would not be joining us at home. She had another home, another set of parents. She had a better life ahead of her, one that would be better than I could ever give her.

My heart began to swell with pain, and my breathing became ragged. I swallowed and took a deep breath, trying to keep the puddles of tears away. My mom told me that the baby could feel my emotions. This little tiny human didn't need to feel them. They hurt too much.

My dad couldn't hold her because the pain of not seeing her until she was older was too much. I needed to hold her because I needed to remember every feeding, every diaper change, and every detail about her so that I could make it through the next 18 years.

The Older Man

Early 2000

"You're the most amazing woman I've ever met," he said. He told me that all the time.

I had a hard time believing him, but I swooned every time he said it. He called me a woman instead of a girl, which I fancied as well.

He picked me up from the end of my driveway that night. Living on a secluded road without very many cars made sneaking out easy. My heart was thumping – it was the first time I had ever done something like that, alone. I snuck out once before with my best friend. I hadn't been as scared with her by my side, but it could have been the moonshine that we shot diluting the fear. This night, I was alone and without the liquor making me invincible.

"I've missed you," he whispered in my ear as he kissed my cheek.

"I've missed you too," I replied sheepishly. I believed the words that left my nervous lips. They seemed real as I spoke them.

Other boys at school never talked to me as he did. They said I was cute, but so and so was cuter, and I was more of a friend than anything. Sure, I was in the eighth grade and shouldn't be too worried about boys, but I was boy crazy. I had a couple of crushes at school, and they didn't seem to be too interested in me. I felt stuck in the friend zone.

This guy, this man, showed me attention and told me everything I ever wanted to hear. He told me I was smart and beautiful. He told me I looked a lot older than I was. He told me I was the only one he could think of.

He was driving down the road, heading toward an old church that was tucked far in the woods. He parked under an old oak, where we would spend our little makeshift date.

After a couple of wine coolers, he started kissing me. The kisses intensified, making my body react in a way I couldn't understand. With his hands all over my body, I started to take off my shirt.

"Are you sure you want to?" He asked quietly.

Kissing him in reply, I nodded my head. I was sure he was the one for me. No other guy ever talked to me like this before. He was sincere, or so I thought.

With my heart racing in the bed of his truck, I undressed with his help. He asked me again if I was sure this was what I wanted. I nodded and gave him the one thing that I could never get back.

The pain wasn't bad. He was easy and treated me like glass. I didn't know what to do. I had heard tales from others who had ventured where I had not. Afterward, he held me for a few hours. We talked about how we wished we could tell the world we were together. I wanted to tell my parents about this wonderful guy, but I knew they would never approve.

Daddy had met him once before when he dropped me off at the movies. It took me forever to talk him into allowing me to go on a date. I told my dad he was 16. I had to do some convincing to let him drop his 14-year-old off, but I finally had him convinced.

I was so excited. It was my first date, ever. "I can wait for him," I told my dad.

"I bet you can. But I want to meet him." Daddy wasn't fond of the date idea at all, and dropping me off before my date arrived was not going to happen.

Finally, I saw him walk across the parking lot. "There he is," I said as I smiled like the schoolgirl I was.

"He doesn't look 16."

My heart started racing, and the only thing I could think of was continuing to convince him that yes, he was 16.

My date walked up to my dad's truck, "Hello, sir."

"Hello, my name's Tim." Daddy glared. "How old are you?"

"I'm 16," he replied.

"What school do you go to?"

"Cherokee High." Glancing past my dad, my date looked at me and smiled. I smiled back, nervous that I wasn't going to be released from the truck.

After more questioning, my dad finally allowed me to get out. I went to the theaters ready to see a movie, and still in shock I pulled off the lie.

"I wasn't sure he was going to let me out," I said as I let out a sigh of relief. "He doesn't believe you are 16."

"How old does he think I am?"

"18."

We laughed because we knew 18 wasn't his age either. What I hated about dating him was that I could never tell my parents the truth. They would never let me see him again if they found out he was 24.

The Scary Truth

I visited my dad's house every other weekend. After sneaking out successfully two weeks before, I was ready to do it again. I was on the phone with Don. "You're gonna come get me tonight?"

"I'm gonna try, baby. No promises, though. Dad said something about needing the truck." Don borrowed his dad's truck, so we were at his mercy. "Do you want to call me later?"

"My dad said I can't be on the phone after nine. He says that most people are normally asleep by then," I sighed.

"I don't know what to do. I want to see you, but it is a long drive if you aren't able to get out, and you won't know if I have the truck or not."

"I know. What if I walk down after my dad and his girlfriend go to bed. I'll wait to see if you can make it?"

"If you want to." He seemed truly sad. "I want to see you again."

"I want to see you too. I miss you." My heart was aching. It had been two weeks of just talking on the phone.

"I miss you too, beautiful."

My heart soared at his words. "I love you."

"I love you, too. I hope I get to see you."

"Me too."

Our conversation ended. It was time for us to get off the phone, and I wasn't sure if we really made a time to meet at the end of the driveway, but I was going to go anyways.

I waited until everyone was asleep and headed for the front door.

"Where are you going?" one of my step-brothers asked.

I jumped and turned to see Steven waiting for an answer. "You know where I am going," I hissed. Steven knew everything except that I was sneaking out tonight.

"When will you be back?" He asked.

I thought his question was ridiculous. "I don't know. Why?"

He shrugged. "I'm just worried."

Confused, I asked, "Worried? Worried about what?"

"You being gone. What if mom or your dad wake up and want to know where you are?"

"I don't know. I doubt they'll wake up, though. Promise me you won't tell on me, please," I pleaded.

"I won't. Just be careful."

I shut the door behind me as quietly as I could. Of course I was going to be careful. I was going to be with Don... I hoped.

I walked to the end of the driveway, hating that I had to sneak behind my parents' backs to see the man I loved. If only I could tell them the truth and they would be alright with it.

I waited for what seemed hours. It looked like he wasn't coming, and I was starting to get discouraged. The chills crept over my body, informing me that I was cold. Knowing I should go ahead and go back in, I decided to give it a few more minutes. I sat listening to the Whip-poor-will bird singing its nightly song and trusting that Don would eventually show up.

"Amanda." A voice broke the silence.

Startled, I turned to see my dad standing behind me. "Hey, Daddy," I said shakily.

"What are you doing? Waiting for that boy?" he asked in a voice I couldn't recognize.

"No, no." I was trembling, terrified about what might happen if he found out I actually was. "I was just sitting here thinking. I couldn't sleep, so I decided to walk a little."

"Well, why don't you go back up to the house," he said in a stern voice.

I could tell it wasn't an option. It was a command, and that was something I didn't get too often from him.

I walked up the long, dark driveway scared to death that Don would pull up. It took me forever to finally fall asleep, but by the time I did, I had yet to hear my dad return from waiting.

The next morning I awoke and had a hard time facing my dad. I didn't want to leave my bedroom, but I also wanted Daddy to believe that I was just out for a walk last night. Fear gripped me every time I thought that Don actually showed up. Finally, I got the courage to walk out to the kitchen and fix a bowl of cereal. As usual, Daddy was out on the porch drinking his coffee.

With the door wide open and the screen door closed, I said, "Good morning, Daddy."

"Good morning." He said it like he said it all his life. No difference, no disappointment, no anger, just his normal greeting.

I went about my morning in the typical fashion. Finally, my dad pulled me to the side.

"I just wanted you to know, he didn't show up," he said matter-of-factly.

"What?" I tried playing dumb.

"That boy," he said, giving me a disapproving look.

"He wasn't supposed to." I was going to stick to my fib as much as possible. However, the fib really wasn't that big since I wasn't sure if he would make it or not. If I was being honest with myself, I had a feeling he wouldn't be there.

The afternoon went on as it usually did. My dad didn't say anything else again about Don, and I kept away from him to ignore any more disapproving glances he might give me.

My three stepbrothers and I decided that a day full of gaming on the PlayStation would be the best way to spend our time. We played "Need for Speed" and "Tomb Raider." My youngest step-brother, Brandon, was the worst at completing the levels, so, being the mean bigger brothers and sister, we took the game system over.

Brandon got so mad at us that he looked at me and screamed, "I'm going to go tell your dad how old your boyfriend is!"

I laughed it off and didn't believe him. Steven and I continued to play the game. Brandon left the room and then the home phone rang. Without caller ID, I wasn't sure who was calling, so I picked it up and said, "Hello."

"I need you to come out to the barn, right now."

It was my dad. The anger in his voice sent chills throughout my body. I couldn't move.

"Who was it?" Steven asked.

"My—my dad," I said in a shaky voice.

Brandon came in seconds after I hung up the phone. I stared him down, "Did you really tell him?" I prayed that the answer was no.

He nodded and my heart sank. "He wants you to come out to the barn." Brandon didn't care. All he cared about was that he got the game system back.

I started crying. There was no hiding. No running away. I had to find the courage and walk to the barn. Each step seemed like it was my last. With the weight of disappointment, shame, and guilt on my shoulders, I walked to the barn.

I entered and looked at the hurt, the anger, and the possible fear on my father's face. The tears started streaming down my cheeks. I didn't know how to handle the stress that I put on myself. Then the fear hit hard like a sledgehammer. My heart raced like it was in the Kentucky Derby .

"Is he really 24?"

I cried. That's all I could do. No trying to figure out a lie to cover up what my dad already accepted as truth. I just sat there and sobbed uncontrollably. I couldn't find the courage to say yes, but saying no would be a lie.

"Call him up and have him come over," I heard my dad say.

I looked at him in disbelief. Why would he be saying something like this? He must have registered the confusion because he repeated himself.

I stood to leave and go inside to call Don. "Don't go anywhere. Sit here and call him."

I sat as commanded. I dialed the number that I had dialed so many times before, except this time, I was terrified what might happen next.

Donald, Don's dad, answered. "C-can I speak to Don?" I asked, trying to control my voice.

"Sure, hold on a minute."

I waited as my dad sat waiting.

"Hey, girl," I heard Don say.

Unable to control my emotions, bursting into another sobbing fit, I managed to say the word, "Hey."

My dad spoke before our conversation went any further. "Hand the phone to me."

I did, and I ran for my life into the bedroom that I hoped would hide me away from the world until my time was near.

Thirty minutes later, my jaw dropped as I watched Don's truck pull up my driveway. Stepping out onto my porch, I saw my dad walking from the barn, motioning for Don to head his way.

"You too, Amanda," my dad added.

Don, only giving me the slightest glance, walked to the barn. I followed, terrified of what was about to take place. Entering the office area of the barn, I noticed a gun leaning on my dad's desk. I sat quietly, not trusting myself to talk.

After what seemed an eternity, my dad spoke. "Y'all need to cut this out. Right here. Right now." He glared at Don. "You're old enough to know why." He nodded toward me. "She is not."

"Yes, sir. I understand," Don replied.

I just nodded my head. There was nothing to say. He was breaking us up, and I couldn't do anything about it.

Before we left, Don asked, "Can I say goodbye?"

With a heavy sigh and my dad's eyes resting on me, he finally huffed out, "Yes."

We took the path from the barn to the back yard, which actually was the beginning of the tree line. Holding hands and walking, we were silent.

Finally, I choked out, "Don, what are we going to do?"

Caressing my hand with his thumb, he asked, "What do you mean?"

"I don't want to stop seeing you or talking to you, but—"

"He said we had to knock it off, but we don't have to stop calling each other."

Nodding, I sighed, "Yeah, but how am I going to see you? I want to see you."

He looked up in deep thought. "You think you can sneak out of your mom's house?"

I shared a room with my little brother. Sneaking out would not be easy. However, there was a door that led out the front of the house in the same room. "I might be able to," I said, unsure of actually pulling it off.

"I will see you again. Don't worry about that." He smiled at me in a way that made butterflies soar through my stomach.

Returning the smile I said, "You think so?" My smile started to falter, "What if he finds out about it?"

"How often do your mom and dad talk?"

"Not much at all. My dad tries to avoid talking to her as much as possible."

"Well, then we should be fine. Besides, he said we needed to stop it here. He didn't say anything about stopping it there." He touched my cheek and held his hand there, all the while staring deep into my eyes.

For an hour we walked the property, not leaving my dad's sight. Within a snap, the time was up. I had to say goodbye, but it wasn't entirely sad. We figured we would see each other by the end of the week if our plan worked. I hugged him. My dad sat patiently watching, fighting his own battle within.

I was quiet the remainder of my time at my dad's house. I did communicate, but it was more a nod or shake in reply to questions. I didn't know what to say, and I was still trying to figure out how I would sneak out of my mom's house.

Finally, my dad was driving me home—a place where I could pick up the phone and call Don with no worries of anyone listening.

Half way to my house, my dad's strained voice broke the silence. "I'm sorry I had to make it end."

I just nodded my head. He thought it was ending, but I knew it wasn't over.

"You'll find a guy that is your age and that will treat you right," he continued, hoping that I would see a positive side of the situation. "He wasn't good for you."

I looked out the window, watching the trunks of the trees meld to-gether as we passed. What could I say? I was lost between trying to be a good girl and trying to be with the man that loved me. Dad's words kept playing in my head, "Y'all need to cut this out. Right here. Right now." I had to remind myself that he was saying here, as in his home. He didn't say anything about my mom's.

Silence fell on us again as we pulled onto the all-too-familiar road that led to my mom's. As we arrived at the house, Dad finally spoke again, "I love you, Amanda."

"I love you, too."

The Secret Life

For the next few months, I continued to sneak out of the house. There were times when my mom and stepdad were still up, but for the most part, they were already asleep. At school, only a couple of friends knew about my after-hour activities and about Don's age. I didn't bother to tell all of my friends about the guy I had fallen for. They wouldn't agree to our meetings or his age.

When Don picked me up, we would travel the roads going anywhere within a 50-mile radius of my house. Sometimes we just drove around. Other nights we stopped and enjoyed each other's company. Some nights, Don would bring food for us to eat. I soaked up every moment that I got to spend with him. I tried to limit my sneaking out to one or two times a week, but it gradually increased to three and sometimes four nights.

I never had any issues with my parents hearing me open the door or my brother waking to the squeaky hinges. However, some nights he would stir for a moment upon my return. Being in a groggy state, he didn't understand what was going on and quickly fell back asleep. I got used to leaving at night and having little to no sleep, so no one ever guessed something was amiss. Dad thought I had stopped all communications with Don, and my mom thought I slept every night. I had it made. The only thing that I hated about my lifestyle was keeping Don secret from almost everyone.

One night when Don was returning me home, my bedroom light was on. My heart stopped. Instead of stopping near the house, per usual, Don continued driving.

"What do I do?" I asked as my breathing became rapid and my heart began to thump out of my chest.

"I don't know." He was in shock, too. Neither of us thought this would ever happen.

Further down the road, he turned around and we headed back to the house. My light was off.

"Do you think it might've been your brother?" He asked.

"Possibly ..." I was scared to return to my room, but I had no choice. I exited the truck and began my walk.

I never had to walk far—normally a couple of driveways. Tonight was no different. I got to the porch and I stood at the door for a moment. Quietly. Listening. I heard nothing. Scraping up a little bit of courage, I opened the door. The room was dark. My brother laid sleeping, as he always did. My heart began to slow, and I thought the light being on was something I imagined. Lying on my bed, I listened to the rhythm of my heart as it finally came to a normal beat. Then, I heard my door open.

"Amanda!" She didn't scream, but it was a stressed whisper. "Where have you been? I've been terrified. I couldn't find you. I called your dad and ..."

My mom was rambling on and on, but the only thing I heard was she called my dad. For a second time that night, my heart stopped. "Why did you call Daddy?"

"Because I was worried sick about you, Amanda. I didn't know what to do. You were gone."

She looked like she wanted to cry, but there was enough bottled anger to keep the tears away. The phone rang, and my mom answered.

"Hey, James... Yeah, she made it back... here she is."

Taking the phone from my mom, I swallowed the lump in my throat. "Hey, Daddy."

"Were you out with Don?" His voice cracked like a whip.

"Yes." The lump was back.

"I told you both to knock it off. Do you know how worried I was? I was about to head there and start searching for you. Why did you disobey me?"

I had no answer but the one Don had me believe. "I thought you meant to quit seeing each other at your house."

"No, Amanda! I told you two it had to stop. Period."

I handed the phone to my mom. My heart was broken. My life was falling apart. I enjoyed my time with the man I loved, even if it was in secret. He listened to me in a way that no one else did. Better yet, he seemed to understand me when I didn't understand myself. I was being forced to stay away from him. I plopped on my bed crying as my heart swelled with pain. Why did life have to be so unfair?

My mom was at my side after she hung up the phone. "Amanda, you know you are going to have to be punished."

Crying into my pillow, I nodded my head.

"I hate that I have to do this." She always told me how much she hated having to make me suffer, but it never made me feel any better.

I didn't sleep much that night. I wanted to sneak off and call Don, but my mom removed the phone in my room when she left.

Being grounded and stuck at home for what seemed forever didn't stop me from trying to contact Don. The only opportunities I had to sneak and call him were when my mom wasn't home. Usually, they were few and far between. Once I finished paying my time, I knew that sneaking out wasn't going to be as easy. Not only was the door leading outside locked and nailed, but my mom also checked on me constantly.

However, since I was no longer grounded, my phone privileges returned. My first call was to Don.

"Hey, how are you?" I asked him, but continued without giving him a chance to answer. "I've missed you so much." It had been over a month since I last saw him.

"I've missed you, too." His voice was wonderful to hear. "How have you been?"

"I've been alright. I'm much better now that I get to talk to you."

As our conversation continued, a question that lingered between us finally floated to the surface. "Are you able to sneak out?" he asked.

"I don't know. My door has been nailed shut, and I can't go out the other door." My heart ached. I felt like my world ended when I told him the slim chances.

"What about the window?"

"I don't—" And like that, the lightbulb went on. The windows were not locked, had no screens, and I thought I might be able to get them open. Our house was old, so the windows sometimes would not open without exerting a lot of force. "Let me call you back in a few."

We got off the phone, and I tried opening the window. It took a bit, but I was elated once I felt it move. I called Don back, and we arranged our plans for the evening.

The Change Within

"Hey, you know that guy over there?" My friend was leaning toward me on the lunch table. It was May. The last month of middle school and the entire eighth-grade class was shuffled into the school's cafeteria. We had a guest coming to talk to us about shifting to high school. Having the entire grade in one area gave us a chance to socialize and see friends we normally didn't get to see every day.

I looked down to where she was pointing and finally zoned in on the guy she was talking about. Brown hair that was barely a half-inch long. "No, but he's cute."

"Well, he knows I know you and wants me to introduce you two," she smiled.

"Really? He really asked you to do that?" I was shocked. This was the first time any guy ever asked about me—well, at least, one that was in school with me.

"Yes, he did. He thinks you're cute and wants your number."

I pulled away from Skyla in shock. "You're kidding, right?"

"No, I'm not. So do you want me to introduce you or not?" She seemed excited.

I thought about it for a good moment. Here this guy was, interested in me and my age. An age that both my parents would approve of, and I would no longer have to sneak out or lie about who I was on the phone with. Playing nervously with my necklace, I weighed the facts in my head. Finally, I looked back at Skyla. "I guess you can introduce me."

My decision was made. I was going to meet this stranger that found me interesting enough to seek out a mutual connection between us.

Not knowing what Skyla had in mind, I watched as she immediately got up and went over to him. I filled my other friends in on what was happening. My palms began to sweat, my heart started beating faster, and I had butterflies fluttering throughout my stomach. Skyla had retrieved the mystery guy, and they were standing before me.

"Amanda, this is Cory. Cory, this is my friend Amanda," Skyla said.

"Hey," I said barely making a noise.

"Hey," he smiled. "How are you?"

"I'm good." He sat down next to me as we waited for the guest speaker to arrive.

We whispered and flirted throughout the entire speech, not really caring what the speaker was saying. He was searching through my book bag, while I doodled on paper. I wasn't sure what he was searching for, but I let him continue the flirtatious act without stopping him. At times, he would steal my pen so he could add his own doodles to mine. With friends around helping the conversation, we didn't have an awkward moment, and I realized I really liked this guy.

As the speech came to an end, a teacher stood up to dismiss us by homerooms. Before Cory had to exit, he grabbed my pen one more time and grabbed a piece of paper. Writing his number and tearing the page in two, he asked for my number as he handed me his.

That night when I got home, I called Cory. I was excited to talk to someone my age. I decided it was time to make a change in my life.

I finally called Don. It took a lot for me to pick up the phone to dial his number. After all, I needed to tell him that I no longer wanted to be his girlfriend.

"Is everything ok?" he asked after our normal hellos.

"Yeah, well—" I paused for a moment. The words were there, but I couldn't speak them. "Don, I was thinking—" another long pause.

"What's wrong?" He knew something had changed.

"I think, maybe, we should stop." I held my breath as I waited for a response.

"Stop? Stop what?"

"Stop seeing each other. Really," I sighed, "you're too old for me, and I'm tired of having to lie to everyone."

I said what I needed to, and silence was my answer. It seemed like it lasted forever.

"Ok," came the reply.

"I'm sorry." I didn't know what else to say. I did feel bad that I was telling him goodbye, but I wanted a change.

"Can I come see you one more time?" He pleaded.

I thought for a moment. It truly wouldn't hurt if he came over and talked for a bit. "Alright, I guess that'll be fine."

About an hour later, Don passed my house. We had already decided that he would park down the road and walk up to the house so I didn't have to actually leave. I opened the window and jumped to the ground that was just about three feet below me. Moments later, I saw Don in the shadows.

"Hey," he said in a low, saddened voice.

"Hey," I said quietly. The nervous butterflies started flying again. I was looking forward to a normal teenage life, a life in which I could ask my parents if I could go out with friends and not have to worry about hiding someone from them. I could be free from the lies I constantly had to memorize. I could be myself again.

On the side of the house below my window, we sat quietly, not sure what to say to one another. Don broke the silence, "I know this is it. But can I ask one more thing from you?"

"Umm, I guess." I didn't know what he would ask of me, but I was willing if it helped him ease his pain.

"Can we do it one more time, so that way I can remember you always?"

The silence became heavy as I thought about it. "I don't know," I huffed.

"Please, Amanda."

"I just ... I want to say yes, but then I also feel like I should say no."

"Please," he begged. "It will make me feel better since you are dumping me."

I already felt bad that I made the decision I did. And yet, I knew it was the right one. Finally, I gave in. "One last time."

He hugged me so tight and laid his jacket down on the ground. He knew I would give in and he came somewhat prepared. I asked if he brought protection. He started looking through his pockets and then picked his jacket back up to do an extensive search. Not finding any protection he confidently told me, "I don't. But it's alright, I'll pull out and everything will be ok."

"Will it?" I was nervous to go any further.

"Yes. Nothing will happen. I promise."

Once again, I trusted him and laid down in hopes that this last time, nothing would happen.

The next morning, I woke feeling like a weight had been lifted off my shoulders. I went to school ready to see the end of another year. I had two vacations this summer. I would be going to California in June, and then I would be going to South Carolina in July.

Shortly after arriving at school, Cory found me at my locker. "How was your night?"

"It was good," I smiled.

"So, I wanted to ask you something," his face started to turn a soft shade of pink.

With butterflies in my stomach, I nodded my head.

"You want to be my girlfriend?" His soft pink went to red, and I'm sure my face was doing the same.

"Yes," I smiled at him as he gave me a hug and walked me to my first class.

The New Life

Summer began, and I didn't have much time for anything. I called Cory when I could, but I was, for the most part, out doing things with family and friends.

By midsummer, I realized I hadn't seen Don in almost two months. I called him very little because it was still awkward to talk to him. In between midsummer and the end of the summer, I noticed that I was missing something. My period. I thought about the last time I had my menstrual, but with so much going on, I couldn't remember. In May, we were being prepared for high school; we constantly had speakers at the school, a weeklong field trip, an eighth-grade dance, and a picnic. Then summer began, which had my days running together.

As the days continued to move forward and I became acclimated to a new school, I began to truly worry about what was going on with my body. I didn't know where to go for help, so I reached out to Don.

"I don't think you're pregnant, but just in case, I'll buy you a test," he told me.

"Will you please?" I was so scared to think about the possibility of me being pregnant. "How will you get it to me?"

"How about I come over tonight? I'll bring the test, and I'll bring some dinner."

I was all for it. "What are you making?"

"Crab legs." I could hear his smile.

"Oh, that would be awesome! Thank you."

Once again, I had to sneak out. I had stopped sneaking out after I told Don it was over. I promised myself that I'd never do it again. However, I never imagined I would need to take a pregnancy test. This needed to be done. I had to find out if there was life growing inside me.

He picked me up, and we traveled down the road to a neighborhood that was in the beginning stages of construction. We decided that eating would be best done first. I didn't want to lose an appetite for my favorite food. Once the crab legs were gone, I knew it was time. Don unpackaged the test and handed it to me.

"What do I do?" I was terrified. It was that moment in which I needed the comfort and support from my mom, but it was an issue I couldn't take to her.

"You just pee on it."

I held the small stick in my hand looking at the small area I had to make sure I hit. It seemed like a simple task for an adult who wanted to see a positive result, but that was not the case for me. It was dark, I had to squat, we were in a vacant cul-de-sac, and the last thing I wanted was for it to be positive. "What if I miss?"

"Then we'll try again later."

My stomach sunk. I wasn't sure if I wanted to see the result or not. What would I do if I was? I did my business and handed the instrument back to Don. Not able to look at the home test, Don watched the stick, waiting for the reply. It took about a minute before the answer was clear on his face.

Looking at his pale face, I said, "Let me see."

He handed the test to me. I began to shake uncontrollably as I looked at the two pink lines. I was 14! I just started the ninth grade. What would I do? I didn't have a job. I didn't have a driver's license. I didn't have a house. All my needs were still provided by my parents.

"What do we do?"

He was quiet for a long moment. He wrapped his arms around me, preparing me for his answer. "We could abort it."

"How are we going to do that?" Backing away from Don's embrace, I wrapped my arms around myself. The air became cold and heavy when moments before it was a mucky 70 degrees. I felt like I was in a nightmare.

"I'll call some clinics tomorrow, and we will get you an appointment."

"Will I need my mom?" I've always had my mom at appointments, so why would this be different? Shaking my head I said, "I can't tell her." She would flip, and I didn't know if I would survive.

"What about your dad's girlfriend?"

Amy would keep quiet, and she could play the role of my mom. I just would have to confess to her. "I can't call her in the middle of the week. It'll look suspicious."

"Well, wait till this weekend then."

And that's what I did. I waited for the weekend. I told her everything. From the sneaking out to what all took place. Amy comforted me and told me she would get me to a clinic. We set up an appointment for a Saturday. Saturday was easiest because she couldn't pick me up any other time. The plan was for her to get up early and take me shopping. In reality, we would meet up with Don.

All went as planned. Amy and I got up and left before anyone else was awake. We met Don and headed to find the abortion office. We drove around the area where the clinic was supposed to be, but we were unable to find it. Stopping at a payphone, Don called the clinic but received no answer. After searching for over an hour and finding out that the only clinic nearby was closed, we decided to call it quits. Not knowing how far along I was, Amy decided I needed to go to the hospital.

I was 12 weeks pregnant.

My first year in high school, and I was walking around pregnant. No one else knew. Cory was excited to see me after our summer break, but I couldn't return his excitement. I began pushing him away. Not wanting to, but not having another option, I told him I didn't really want to date him. I felt like a horrible person and wanted to protect him from me. Once he found out my secret, he wouldn't want to talk to me anyway. I thought he might view it as I cheated on him. In a way, I felt like I did. It also wouldn't be too much longer and people would notice that I was tainted.

I continued to talk to Don about finding another clinic, but we couldn't find another time.

At school, all I wanted to do was sleep. My body seemed to be always exhausted. Once I got home, I was curled up in my bed sleeping. It never failed; I needed a nap every day. If I wasn't napping, I was searching AOL for what was happening inside my body.

One day after school, my mother came into my room. Upset that I was taking a nap, she asked a question I wasn't expecting. "Are you smoking pot?"

I was shocked that she would ask me a question like that. "What?" I've never had the urge to smoke pot, and here my mom thought I was. "Why would you think that?"

Her voice lowered a notch, "When I was in ninth grade, I smoked pot and would come home every day and take a nap," she paused for a moment. "The same thing you are doing."

I was shocked because I was being falsely accused and shocked to find out that my mom had smoked pot. I wondered if she would be happy to find out what was really making me so fatigued or if she would wish it was drugs. "Mom, I'm not doing pot." I was firm in my answer. I wanted to make sure she knew that I meant it. I didn't want her to question me any further. It worked for a few days.

The following week she asked me again. This time, I couldn't convince her. She was threatening to give me a drug test so she would know for sure. She wouldn't accept my answer, and I was becoming frustrated with her accusations.

"Mom, I'm not smoking pot," I said once again. The time had come to confess why I was always tired. I walked over to my desk in my room. Under a ton of other books and loose paper, I found my diary. Within it was a paper that I handed my mom. I watched her face as she read the report the hospital sent home with me. In a hushed tone, I reassured her, "I'm not smoking pot."

She looked at me. Traumatized. Not sure what to say to me, she just continued to stare. I had shown her something she never expected. In her mind, it was a freak accident never meant to happen to her baby. That's what I was, even at 14 years old. I was and will always be her baby.

Within the next couple of days, Mom scheduled an appointment for me. Lost in what she was supposed to do, she was hoping the doctor would be able to guide her.

"What options do we have?" My mom asked the doctor.

"She could continue with the pregnancy, or she could abort the fetus," the Doctor said.

My hand went to my stomach, and I looked at my mom.

"When do we have to decide by?" my mom asked. She was fighting a battle inside herself. I could see her struggling.

"In the state of Georgia, a mom can abort as late as 22 weeks." The doctor looked between the two of us. "I'll step out and let you two discuss the options."

I thought about it for a little bit, and I thought about the information I read online. "Mom, this little life within me is already able to recognize my touch and can hear my voice, and the baby continues to grow."

My mom nodded. She understood; this was not just a fetus growing inside of me. It was a baby. A little boy or a little girl.

Then I remembered a poem I read recently:

"ABORTION – A POEM

They don't know I can hear them, as they argue once again.
My Mom and Dad are yelling, saying, 'what if it's a sin?'
I hear my Father pacing, as he walks across the room,
But, I am safe and cozy here inside my Mother's womb.

In four more months, I'm going to see, the look upon their face,
But, now I am still growing, as I look around this place.
I have all my fingers, and I see all of my toes,
I think that I am perfect, as my little body grows.

They don't know I'm a little girl, I hope they are surprised,
I can't wait to see the happy look that's in their eyes.
I know that I have sisters, and I know I have a brother,
I wonder what they meant by, 'we just can't afford another.'

I hear my Daddy saying, 'the appointment is tomorrow.'
Then he walked out and all I'm feeling now is Mommy's sorrow.
It's late as I can feel my Mommy crawling into bed.
I wonder why she's crying, as I feel her pat my head.

Oh well, it's time to go to sleep, she's laying on her back.
I feel so comfortable tonight, I don't think I'll attack.
Sometimes when she is on her back, it doesn't feel quite right,
And sometimes all that I can do is toss and turn all night.

But I am comfortable tonight, so I can get some sleep,
And as I slowly close my eyes, I hear my Mother weep.
Then suddenly I hear my Dad say, 'wake up sleepy head,
We're going to the doctor's office, so get out of bed.'

It is early morning, and I slept all through the night,
But now I feel my Mother tensing, something isn't right.
I hear my Daddy saying, 'time to get that baby out,'
And now I become worried, as I hear my Mother shout.

I must have been mistaken, and I must have counted wrong,

Could it already be nine months? It didn't seem that long.
I've heard them talk "cesarean" my brother came that way,
If that is how I will be born, this is my lucky day.

Now I hear more voices, of a doctor and a nurse,
But, wait a minute, I feel pain and it is getting worse.
What is going on, I want to see my Mom and Dad,
But all I feel is pain and it is really getting bad.

I'm starting to get woozy, I hope this is over soon,
I see the light as I am being dragged out from the womb.
I'm losing strength, I can't go on, my body is so weak,
And now there's nothing left to do, so I drift off to sleep.

Then suddenly I am awake, now what's that beating sound,
I do not see my Mom and Dad, they're no where to be found.
The pain is gone, and I feel like I'm flying through the air,
And I am in the arms of someone, that must really care.

I feel the tender arms I'm in, and I feel so much love,
And then I realize, they are the angels from above.
My mind is so confused, and all my thoughts need to be sorted,
But then I understand, when one of them whispers, 'aborted.'"
Author Unknown

There was a knock on the door, and the doctor walked back in. I looked at her and shook my head. "I'm too far along. The baby already knows my touch and knows who I am. There's no way I could go through with it."

My mom nodded in agreement. Leaving the office, my mom wrapped me in a big bear hug. It was a hug full of relief and full of fear. We knew that the next few months would be challenging even though neither of us knew exactly what was in store for me.

The Truth Revealed

I knew what had to be done. My pregnancy was due to my irrespon-sibility, and now I needed to accept the trials that were ahead. I called Don and we discussed him getting us a place to live together. I could still go to school, and he would work to provide for us. At least, that was our game plan. He already had a couple of places picked out. One was an apartment above a garage—he knew the owner. Another option was getting an apartment in Canton. Either way, he was positive that he could provide for three.

Telling family and friends about the pregnancy wasn't going to be easy, but it was my next step. The first person on the list was my dad. I looked for help from my dad's girlfriend in order to tell him. We decided to start from the absolute beginning and tell him about the first attempt at hiding the soon-to-be bulge.

He was sitting when I told him. Shocked, he asked, "Amanda, what are you going to do?"

I shrugged my shoulders. I knew what Don and I discussed, but I wasn't sure how Daddy would take the news.

"Babies are not cheap. What about your schooling?" He continued to ask questions one after the other without pause for me to answer. He was clearing them from his head and wanting me to think about them before I gave an actual answer. Then he asked a question with a pause afterward, "What does Don think?"

I confided in him the discussion Don and I had. Then my dad had another question. "Where does he work?"

"Lowes."

He turned his head up to the sky asking God to help him keep his cool. Looking back at me he responded, "Y'all are not going to be able to afford a house and a baby on his salary, Amanda."

I heard my dad, but all I could think of was what Don said. He said he could provide, and I believed him.

Weeks had gone by after the discussion between my dad and me. My parents contacted the Cherokee and Forsyth police agencies to report Don for sleeping with and manipulating a minor. They also contacted my school, which needed to be informed of my pregnancy.

I would not be moving in with Don, per my dad who kept repeating to me that Don would never be able to provide for us as he should. I felt lost as my dad's words sunk in. I was stuck just taking each day one at a time. I felt ashamed that I let my entire family down. I felt like a disappointment to all my friends, and they didn't even know what had happened, yet.

My two best friends at school were Brittany and Becca. I told Brittany first. I figured she would handle my situation better than Becca. She didn't push me away, and she was still my friend. When I told Becca, it was difficult to get the words out of my mouth.

"Becca, I have to tell you something," I said one morning on the bus.

"Ok," she replied, waiting for me to go on.

"I—I," I began to stumble. How was I going to tell her? "You know that guy, the one I was dating?"

"Yeah..."

"Well, he and I did some things, and well now... I didn't think it could happen to me, but it did." It was so hard to tell her, and I didn't know why. I knew she would still be my friend, but I was scared how she would handle the news.

She just looked at me, confused. She was patiently waiting for the direct answer.

"I'm pregnant," I finally said in a small whisper.

She looked at me in disbelief, not sure if she had heard me right. I nodded my head. She couldn't say anything in return. She was acting the same way I did a month ago. She couldn't believe it, but she didn't push me away. She was there for me, just like Brittany.

Before long, the rest of my close friends found out, and the rest of the family did too. I received calls constantly and received support from everyone. Not necessarily supporting me to have the child, but support that let me know my family was not going to abandon me. The only thing missing was Don, who now resided in the Cherokee detention center. Even though we were no longer a thing, I still missed talking to him.

One night, my dad came to visit me to see how I was doing. He brought me a package to open. I was excited to get a gift, which was the last thing I would have expected. I opened up the item to discover it wasn't a gift for me. It was a two-pack pacifier set and a pack of diapers.

"This is what you'll have to buy constantly," he told me.

"Okay," I replied, not sure where he was going with his lesson.

"You know how much this cost?"

I shook my head.

"Look on the back of the diapers," my dad said. "There is a receipt."

I turned it over and saw the Walmart receipt. The total read $14.93.

"The pacifiers you might not have to buy so much, but the diapers you will have to buy every week. Sometimes twice, sometimes three times a week. That's $20 to $30 dollars a week on just diapers, Amanda."

I nodded my head. That wasn't too expensive.

"And then on top of that, you have to buy formula, which costs even more than diapers. You're looking at almost $50 to $60 dollars a week. That's $200 to $240 dollars a month. Sometimes more." He looked at me, saddened by the reality he was trying to make me see. "Babies aren't cheap, baby." He wrapped me in a hug.

The baby growing inside of me wasn't a Baby Alive Doll, and my dad wanted me to see the reality of having a child. This was a real baby. A tiny life that would look to me for care.

The Other Option

Lying in bed, I could hear my mom on the phone with someone. Normally, I wouldn't bother to listen in, but I heard my name. Whoever my mom was on the phone with, they were discussing the pregnancy. I ventured into the dining room where my mom sat at the table. It was my grandma on my dad's side. I had three different grandmas. Two lived in California. The other one lived near me in Georgia, which happened to be the grandmother my mom was talking with. My parent's had known for a month, but I hadn't talked to her about what happened because I was terrified to tell her. She was my favorite grandma until I did something wrong, and then I wanted to run. Heaven forbid she request that I take a ride with her. A ride consisted of sitting and listening to her or jumping out of the moving vehicle.

Seeing me walk in, my mom told grandma, "here she is," and handed the phone to me.

My throat was dry. "Hi, Grandma."

"Hello," came a voice that didn't sound happy.

"How are you?" I asked.

"I'm good. How are you?"

"I'm alright." The silence became louder as I waited for her lecture.

"I heard you did some things you shouldn't have." This is how her lectures always started.

"Yeah." I kept my eyes focused down on my feet, hoping the conversation would be over soon.

"So, what are you going to do?"

Holding back the tears, I said, "Keep the baby."

Keeping the baby meant that my future was nothing but unanswered questions. Would I finish high school? Could I get a job? Would my parents help?

"That's a big responsibility for such a young girl. Where are you going to get the money for formula and diapers?" Here voice had yet to lose its edge.

"I'll get a job."

"So you're willing to pay for daycare?"

I hadn't thought about daycare. "No, I thought, maybe, my mom—"

"Amanda, your mom has to take care of her own family. She doesn't have time to take care of another child."

"I know." The silence grew once more between us.

"And you're 14. How are you going to take the baby to doctor appointments? How are you going to get to your job? Are you going to complete high school?"

"I want to finish school." There was more silence. She didn't speak, letting me think about the questions she just asked.

"You have other options—"

It was my turn to cut my grandma off. "Abortion isn't an option."

"I'm glad," her voice finally started to soften, "but you still have another option."

"I do?"

"You can put the baby up for adoption." Her voice lost its edge completely. She was speaking in a tone that was full of love.

"Adoption?"

"Yes. I'm sure there is a family out there that would love to have a baby but can't on their own."

Adoption. Giving my child up. How could I? This was my baby.

"Think about it," she said. "It's best for you, for the family, and for your baby. Amanda, you are too young to take care of a small human." She paused for a moment. "I love you."

"I love you, too." I didn't know what else to say to her, so I handed the phone over to my mom.

I went and sat on my bed, waiting for my mom to come and talk to me. I didn't want to do adoption. This baby was mine. My mom entered the bedroom and sat beside me.

"You know, it's an option I didn't think of." She wrapped an arm around me pulling me close. "You wouldn't have to quit school."

I didn't say anything. I just sat and listened to my own selfish thoughts; I can keep the baby and complete school. I knew I could do it, and I didn't need any help.

"You know a baby is a lot of work. You had me wanting to toss you out a window when you were one-month old."

I looked up in surprise.

"You kept crying and crying. I couldn't get you to sleep. I told your dad if he didn't get up and get you, I was throwing you out the window."

"Did he?" She nodded, and I laughed a little. "Well, I'm glad he got up and got me."

"Me too," She smiled, but it was a sad smile. "Think about adoption. You're too young to take care of a baby. You're just a baby too."

Weeks later, my mom took me to a place in town called Cumming Care Center, a nonprofit organization that helped families. They worked with young pregnant moms, families with little education, and low-income. The facility also offered open adoption.

Before arriving to the center, my mom told me that adoption was the only way. Arguing with my mom, I told her I did have an option and that I wouldn't go through with it. I'm not sure when she changed her mind, but she was becoming more forceful with the adoption idea.

The first meeting was to discuss the adoption process. I sat down with a husky lady that would be helping us with the entire process.

"So who gave you the idea for adoption?" The woman behind the desk asked me.

"My grandma."

Then my mom added, "She doesn't know if she wants to give the baby up."

"Why don't you?" The woman directed at me.

My mom started to answer, but the lady stopped her. "This has to be her decision. Even though she is still a minor, she is the mother of the baby."

As my eyes widened at this revelation, I answered, "Because the baby is my baby." My hand went instinctively to my stomach. I had started to feel the movements and enjoyed every little flutter.

"I understand," she smiled. "How are you going to take care of the baby at such a young age?"

I answered the question as I had answered everyone else.

The woman nodded, accepting my answer. "Don't you want your baby to have a good life and not have to worry about anything?"

I nodded my head. I did want my baby to have the best life possible.

She arched an eyebrow. "Do you think you can give him or her that?"

She let me sit in silence with my own thoughts.

"Why don't you look at some profiles of couples that are looking to adopt? Some people aren't able to have kids, so all they can do is hope for a mother to come along who picks adoption for her unborn child."

"I know that if I do decide adoption, it'll be to a family that can't have kids," I said.

The lady smiled. "Alright, well let me give you some profiles, and you can view them in this room over here."

We got up, and she walked me down the hall to the next room. There was a small love seat and a crib. With blue walls and pale blue carpet, it looked like a nursery room for a little boy. I sat down with five different binders that held the lives of different couples who were looking for a child to fulfill their family. Three of the families had already had their own children or had previously adopted. Placing their profiles to the side, I had only two that I considered possible candidates for my unborn child.

One lived in North Georgia, and the other lived in Oregon. Torn with whom to choose, I read their profiles and discovered that both couples had fertility issues and would never be able to get pregnant. My stomach jumped, and my hand went to my belly. I felt sorry for these women. They would never be able to feel the flutters of a baby inside their wombs.

I got up and headed back to the room where I had sat with the counselor. She looked at me, wondering if I had decided.

"If I were to pick one, I've narrowed it down to two couples."

"That's fantastic." She seemed happy that I had participated, but I didn't feel her happiness. I felt lost.

"But, I'm not sure who I would choose."

She nodded in understanding. "Well, you still have time to decide, and if you want to, you can meet with the parents before choosing. You will be coming back, and we can talk more then."

My mom reached over and patted me on the leg once we got in the car. "It's for the best, baby."

"But this baby is mine."

Frowning, she added, "But you know you won't be able to raise a baby by yourself."

"What about you? Won't you help me?"

"Amanda, we can't afford to take care of a baby."

"But I thought you would help me."

"I can only help you so much," my mom huffed. "You will need to work and support the baby, and then if you want to finish school, you'll be working and going to school. And there won't be going out and having fun with your friends."

"I want to keep my baby," I said with a raised voice to the floorboard of the car.

Taking a deep breath, my mom said, "Amanda, you have to give the baby up for adoption. You don't have a choice."

"Yes, I do. The lady said so."

"No. You don't." I heard the warning in my mom's voice.

I nodded my head and thought back to a video we watched in health. I was trying to block her out and put myself anywhere else but next to her in the confined space of the car. The video that was replaying was of teen parents and their struggles through their teenage years. They went to school during the day, worked in the evening, got their baby to sleep, and then they did their homework. They didn't go out on the weekends, and the only time they saw their friends was in school. They were so busy taking care of their child, they never had time to spend with friends due to school and work. That teenager would soon be me, but I knew I could do it. Then I thought about the moms who never saw their kids, or only saw them for a short time every day. That mom would be me, too. Did I want that for my baby? My heart ached for the right thing to do.

The Changing Lifestyle

Doctor visits had become the usual, and I was informed that they would become more common as I progressed in the pregnancy. I enjoyed my visits to the doctor. Most of the time I got to hear a heartbeat, which made me feel closer to the little human growing inside me.

The day I found out the sex of my baby was the day I became even more attached.

"It's a girl," the sonographer said.

My heart swelled watching the baby move on the screen. She would bounce and her heartbeat would be clear one moment and then muffled by her movement the next.

Tears in my eyes, I looked at my mom. "It's a girl."

She nodded with tears that glistened on her cheeks.

After the ultrasound was finished, we sat in a room with a doctor who went over the usual findings. "Everything else looks good. She's healthy, and we seem to be right on target for her due date."

She was due February 25.

Beyond the doctor visits, I had other responsibilities that I was forced to attend.

My parents pressed charges against Don for child molestation and child manipulation in two different counties, meaning that I had to give my testimony. Twice.

My first testimony took place in Cherokee County. They have a division that is dedicated to making sure that children feel safe when they are interrogated. That is, if you are a little child. For a teenager on the brink of adulthood, it was awkward.

The room I entered was much like an elementary school library. It had children's books and stuffed animals in a corner. There was a mural of Noah's Ark on the wall, and there was a mirror in the room. In the middle of the room was a table that had chairs big enough for an eight-year-old. My parents were shown the room but not allowed to be present during my interview. It was only me and a child advocate.

"You see that mirror?" The child advocate asked me.

I nodded.

"The detectives are behind it," the man in the three piece-suit said. "They can hear and see everything, even if you can't hear or see them."

Taking a seat in the tiny chair, the man began his interrogation. "How did you meet Don?"

"Through a friend."

"How old is your friend?"

"15." Even though the room was to make children feel comfortable, my hands were sweaty and my heart was racing.

"How did he know your friend?"

I gulped. "They're family."

"How did you meet him?"

I ducked my head down. I didn't want to tell him.

"Amanda, it's okay to feel scared, and you may not want to tell me, but you need to. I won't hurt you or be upset with you. Now tell me, how did you meet him?"

"It was one night when I was over at my friend's house." I purposely left out the fact that we snuck out that night to meet him. I didn't want her in trouble.

"Did you have sex with Don?"

Looking down, I nodded. It was hard for me to talk to an adult about having sex and even harder to talk to a total stranger about it.

"Did he force you?"

I shook my head.

"Why did you do it?"

Still looking down, I answered, "Because I love him."

He continued to ask me more questions, and sometimes someone would knock on the mirror. The advocate would exit the room and return to ask more questions. Finally, after receiving vague answers, the detectives decided to end the questioning.

After the interrogation in Cherokee County, my mom took me to be questioned by Forsyth County. If I was uncomfortable in Cherokee, then I was being tortured in Forsyth. The building, in general, was dark. The detective, a short, stocky woman, took me to a room that had carpeted everything: the floors, the walls, and ceiling. The room held two chairs and a video camera.

Taking a seat, the detective began asking me questions. Some were the same as the advocate in Cherokee; some were different. After several questions, the detective and her unsmiling face left the room. I sat looking around, waiting for the walls to start creeping in on me. Once the detective returned to the room, she started asking questions that made me uncomfortable.

"What is oral sex?" she asked.

"Oral sex?" I laughed a little. What did this answer have to do with anything?

"You won't believe how many different answers we get."

I sat looking at her loathsome face and finally answered her. "Oral sex is when you perform sex orally."

After asking a few more questions, she finally escorted me back to where my mom was waiting for me.

If I hadn't been questioned enough about my current state, the school counselor asked me even more questions. We met on a weekly basis for a while. Sometimes my parents were there, and other times it was just the two of us.

Finally, the questioning of what happened came to a stop. I had no more meetings with the detectives, and the counselor moved forward. She only wanted to know how I was currently doing, not what had happened already. My story was out there, at least as much as I was willing to tell. Don had been arrested and was awaiting a trial. When the trial would be, I didn't know. I cried when I found out he was in jail. How were we supposed to get a place? How could he support us?

On top of the arrest, my body was changing. My breasts were getting bigger, and they were becoming sore. My pants got tighter. The clothes my parents bought me before school started were now useless. I started wearing sweatpants and any stretchy pants I could find. I found shirts that would generally be too big and would wear them. My mom took me to find a coat as the days got colder. I found one that fit and went up two sizes. It was a puffy marshmallow-type coat. At first, it swallowed me whole, but I knew I would eventually grow into it. Finally, maternity clothes were handed down to me. I was excited to put them on, especially the blue jeans with the expandable middle.

I was finally able to feel somewhat comfortable in clothes. However, the clothes accentuated the baby bump. I was fine with the bump when I wasn't in school. Everyone knew outside of school. It was when I was in school that I tried my best to hide my secret. I would wear my coat all the time. It didn't matter if the classroom was scorching; my coat kept my secret safe.

Constant meetings that involved the presence of both my mom and dad caused my dad's relationship with his girlfriend to be bumpy. It was so hectic that I wasn't allowed to go to his house on the weekends anymore. If I wanted to see him, he had to come get me, and that was exactly what he did. He would come get me and take me places, and our days were spent driving everywhere.

Once I turned 15, Daddy took me to the DMV so I could get my learner's permit. I was so excited the morning he picked me up. All I could focus on was being able to drive home. Before the written test, I had to take an eye test. I placed my forehead on the vision screener. I was so nervous that I called out a random number, a number that wasn't even in the sequence. The woman at the counter laughed a little but allowed me to start again.

Passing the vision test, I sat down to a computer. I started the first of two tests, which was the road signs. I passed with no problems. The second test started, which was multiple choice. Reading the questions, I tried thinking back to my book, but for some reason, the answers didn't come to me. The questions were confusing, and I felt myself becoming more upset and unsure of the answers I gave.

Before I could answer all the questions, the test ended. I had failed. My dad was the one that would be driving home. It was a quiet ride. Daddy tried to lighten the mood by teasing me, but it didn't make me feel any better. Failure didn't come easily to me, and I felt that I had failed in so many other aspects of my life. My teenage years had just begun, and I had already done a magnificent job at obliterating them.

The Teenage Struggles

I continued to be called out of class randomly to see my school counselor. She knew the plan my mom had for me was to give my baby up for adoption. She also knew that my plan was to raise my baby. She would always ask if I had changed my mind, and I would tell her "no."

"Amanda," she said one morning, looking at me with pity-filled eyes. "You need to really give this more thought than what you have."

"I've given it plenty of thought. I made the mistake, and now I need to own up to my responsibility."

"Yes, but you're still a child. Anyway," she quickly continued, "one day soon, another lady will be coming to talk to you. She is a mentor, and you will be having meetings with her."

I looked at my counselor, confused. Why would someone else need to talk to me? I was tired of having to talk to people. "Who is she?"

"Her name is Laura, and she is a mentor from this area."

I nodded, not entirely happy with the unfolding events.

"You might find that you really like her, and, even better, you might find that y'all have something pretty close in common."

"Really? Was she a pregnant teen?" I asked.

"No," she said and didn't add a comment. She was looking at me for a response.

I lifted my head, giving a half nod. "Oh," was all I could think to respond.

My counselor began to smile. "Her mom was the young teen, and she was given up for adoption."

Two days passed before I was called to the office again. I walked in and gave the receptionists the note that excused me from class. Instead of telling me to go ahead and walk toward my counselor's office, she pointed to a lady that was sitting in a chair where students would sit and wait until it was their turn to see a counselor.

A beautiful brown-haired woman with brown eyes was looking at me and smiling. "Are you Amanda?" she asked.

I nodded.

Looking past me, she asked the receptionist where a quiet place was that we could go sit and talk. We went into one of the school's office meeting rooms where it was just Laura and me sitting at a table that was for about twenty people.

That day, I found out why Laura's mom gave her up for adoption. Her mom was young and couldn't provide for a baby. Laura was placed up for adoption and raised by a family that gave her the life where she was provided for, and she never had to worry about shelter or her next meal. Once Laura was old enough, she looked for her mom.

"We're like best friends," Laura said, talking about her biological mother.

"Really? Was it awkward when you met her?"

She smiled at the memory before she began to reply, "Not at all. We acted as if we knew each other our entire lives."

If I gave up my child for adoption, I wondered if our reunion would be the same. "Do you see her often?"

Laura nodded. "I see her a lot, her and my other siblings. I got to discover this entire family I never knew I had. We gather at family functions, and we are as close-knit as I am with my family."

Starting to see adoption as a possibility, I asked, "If I gave up my baby for adoption, do you think it would be the same?"

Reaching over and patting my hand in an encouraging way, Laura said, "I don't know. Each situation is different, but I have to believe that she will understand that you were young and gave her the chance at a better life, better than what you could have provided."

I gave Laura a hug that day after we talked for almost an hour. When she would visit the school, about once a week, we would discuss more memories of her biological family and her adoptive family. She shared all the joy she got from having two families. We also talked about our faith and Jesus. As we discussed different stories in the Bible, I found my faith growing with her guidance.

Besides trying to live as much of a normal teenage life as I could, I continued to try to get my learners. Once again, my dad took me, and once again, I failed. I was devastated. How could I fail the test twice? I answered to the best of my knowledge, and I was confident that I knew everything there was in the driving book, but I was walking away from the DMV empty-handed.

"It's alright." My dad hugged me. "You'll get your learners. You just have a lot going on and a lot to deal with." I nodded into his shoulder trying to fight back the tears.

My parents decided that I needed to wait a while before attempting to get my learners. I took the news badly, but there was nothing I could say to persuade them to otherwise.

Meanwhile, I decided between the two set of adoptive parents I wanted to adopt my child. Visiting the non-profit organization once again, I found out that one of the two families I had looked at had updated their profile. They recently adopted and now had kids of their own. That left only one choice. I had the option to meet them before I decided, so we tried to arrange a date.

The parents lived in Oregon, which made the arrangements difficult. They had made plans to be in Georgia around Christmas to visit family. However, the only week they were in town happened to be finals week.

We opted to wait until closer to the baby's due date for a meeting.

Outside of adoption, mentors, counselors, and pregnancy, I was thrilled when I got the chance to do normal things with my friends. Going to the movies and hanging out with them was one of our favorite norms.

"Hey, my mom said I could go to the movies," I told Brittany one night over the phone.

"Awesome. We are about to leave, so we will pick you up in a little bit."

I was excited to go see a movie with my friends. It seemed like forever since we went out somewhere together. We were going to see the new movie The Grinch with Jim Carry. Growing up, the cartoon had been a favorite, and thirty minutes was never enough, so I would watch it twice. This new rendition had a running time of almost two hours.

Sitting with a bucket full of popcorn and cookie dough bites, we watched. I enjoyed every minute until Cindy Lou Who started singing, "Where are you Christmas?" I started to get choked up. I was wondering the same thing. Christmas this year didn't feel like Christmas. The magic was gone, the excitement was not there, and I really didn't want anything. The only thing I wanted for Christmas was to be a normal teenager, but I also wanted to raise the baby that was growing within me.

I placed my hand on my large protruding stomach. I was two months away from my due date.

I still found it strange that there was a living human inside my belly. This little one caused me to feel so different and so distant from my friends. They were there for me. I could tell them anything, but they would never truly understand. No one would. Not even older adults who had babies. They never had a baby at 15. More and more people at school found out about my pregnancy. Cory even heard the whispers. He would walk up to me as we passed in the hall and rub my belly. He never asked me questions about the pregnancy. He would just ask if I was feeling alright, and that was about the extent of our conversations. Others that found out didn't take the news as well as Cory. My friend

Ken, in particular, wasn't happy at all.

"Are you mad at me?" I asked him one day as he was trying to avoid me. We had been friends since the second grade and never had a problem talking at all, but ever since I confided in him about the pregnancy, he started giving me the cold shoulder.

"Yes." He walked faster pulling away from me.

Trying to keep up with his pace, I asked, "Why?"

He whirled around facing me. Hurt was all over his face, "It was stupid of you, dating a much older guy and then having sex." His anger stung deeply.

"I thought you said you would always be there for me." He made the promise to me in eighth grade. We were dancing when he told me. I felt elated knowing that I would always have him to look after me. My pregnancy changed everything. All of a sudden, he didn't care about me.

Anger swam in his eyes. "I didn't think you would do something like this." He waved a hand toward my belly.

I stopped and watched him walk away. Eventually, Ken found another way to go to class, avoiding me as much as possible.

Toward the end of my pregnancy, while in one of my classes, all students were asked to stand up next to their chairs. It was a game, and I had to participate. As the game came to an end, people would sit down. I was one of the last ones standing and I started to hear whispers that hurt.

"Is she pregnant?" I heard some say.

"She's gotten really big, really fast," others would say.

Still forced to stand, I stood listening to the comments that pierced my ears. It didn't matter how low the others spoke, I could hear them as if they were screaming. My exposed self was hurting, and I had no place to hide. Already tucked into a shell, I tried to tuck myself even further.

The next morning, I begged my mom to keep me home. I was relieved when she finally said yes. Ironically, that evening I started having contractions. Calling the doctor, my mom was advised to head toward the hospital in Atlanta. The next call was to my dad. We waited for him to arrive, so we could all go to the hospital at the same time.

The hospital was about thirty minutes away with no traffic. Once we got there, my dad dropped us off at Labor and Delivery. After my mom talked to one nurse in triage, I was placed in a wheelchair.

Sitting down, the lady asked me, "What's your date of birth?"

"October 28, 1985."

"Thank you." She placed a hospital band on me, and we began our journey through the hospital labyrinth.

I was placed in a room where they monitored the baby's heartbeat along with the contractions. I laid there terrified. I might be giving birth today, but it was almost a month in advance. Why would she come early? I hadn't even met the adoptive parents yet. Would they be ready for her? Would I be ready to say goodbye?

My dad walked through the door. He had parked the truck as close as possible, but when you are set to deliver at "baby central," parking was sure to be far away.

"Has the doctor been in?" Concern wrinkled his face.

"No," my mom answered. "He is on the way."

Coming over to me, he kissed me on the forehead, "How are you?"

"I'm alright." I tried for a full smile, but I was terrified, so I mustered up the best smile I could give.

And I was alright. The contractions were Braxton Hicks, but the fear was still there. We were released from the hospital within a couple of hours and set to head home. What I felt was my body preparing for labor. I would be giving birth soon, and I would leave empty-handed.

The next day, my dad called to check on me. "Hey, Daddy."

"Hey," I heard him choke. "How are you, baby girl?"

"I'm better." He didn't reply, but I heard his breathing become heavy, and then even heavier. It was a sound I'd never heard out of him. "Daddy, are you ok?"

"Baby," he started to sob even worse. "A train hit us."

"A train hit us?" I was confused. Did a real train hit my dad?

"Yes, a train. Not a real one." He took a deep breath. "A train, baby. It tore right through us and made a huge wreck."

I started crying. He was talking about a train that hit the entire family—this unplanned pregnancy and all the trials that have come with it. The figurative locomotive knocked us all down, and we were trying to figure out how to survive it.

"I'm coming over. I love you." He hung up the phone and arrived about thirty minutes later.

I ran out to greet him as I've always done. He wrapped both his arms around me in a bear hug and squeezed as he started crying again. I was his baby girl who was about to have a little one. I was going through body changes that 15-year-olds shouldn't. I was the one he loved unconditionally, and even though I disobeyed him, he would continue to love me, no matter what. Hearing him cry was something that was foreign to me. This was only my second time hearing it, and it cut to the core. I felt selfish and unworthy. It was my fault that he was crying. I was causing this agonizing pain, and not only for him, but I was the cause of my mom's pain, as well.

I didn't want to see my parents like this. It was my fault they were feeling like their world had been train-wrecked.

Through the tears and the scratchy throat, I said, "I'm sorry."

His hug relaxed a little bit. "I better not squeeze you so much, you might end up in labor."

The Trial Begins

February 2001

I had to go testify against Don before a judge and jury. I didn't want to. Seeing him scared me. Truthfully, I didn't want to tell strangers about our time together with him in the room.

"There will be a child mediator there for you," mom said. She was talking about the trial that was coming up.

"What does that mean?"

"You'll be in a separate room, and when it is time for you to speak, the mediator will appear and speak on your behalf." She smiled and then wrapped her arms around me. The fear was glued to me, and she noticed.

"So I won't have to see him?"

"You might have to see him on a TV screen. They might have a live viewing from the room you'll be in, so you can see what is going on."

Wrapped in my mom's arms, I tried not to think about the trial. I ventured deep into my mind and thought about my happy spot. I thought about swimming in the river with my friends. We spent all day there jumping off rope swings and different size edges. It was our summer escape, and today it was my escape from the problems within.

"Do you think you'll be ready for tomorrow?"

Feeling my body tense up, I replied, "It's tomorrow?"

My mom nodded as I began to cry on her shoulder. Truth is, I wasn't ready, but I had no choice.

I watched TV the remainder of the day to escape my fearful reality; my thoughts constantly caused my stomach to ache and impaled my heart with daggers. As night crept in, I was finally able to sleep, until a stabbing pain caused me to wake.

I walked to my mom's room and slightly pushed on her shoulder, "Mom," I whispered. "My back hurts, really bad."

"Huh," she said trying to gather her surroundings.

"My back, mom. It hurts so bad."

She popped up and started firing off questions, "Is it contractions?"

"No, I don't think so."

"Are you gassy?"

"Well, I feel like I need to go poop, but I can't. And it might be gas. I'm not really sure. I've never felt pain like this."

"Where is the pain at?"

I placed my hand on my lower back and showed her the entire area that was hurting. It was my complete lower back, and it hurt to stand and walk.

"Let's get you lying back down." I nodded and headed back to my room.

I laid back down and found the most comfortable position was on my side. My mom grabbed the phone and made a call to the doctor. She came in pacing back and forth while she waited for a return call.

"I had back labor with you," she said to me while watching the floor.

"But it's too early for me to be in labor."

My mom shook her head. "No, honey. You could actually go anytime. You are considered full-term now."

"You don't think I am in labor, do you?"

"No, well, yes. That's why I want to talk to the doctor first."

I nodded as she rubbed my back. "Please stop." I placed my hand on hers. The rubbing only made it worse.

"Oh, I'm sorry baby." She pulled her hand away and looked down at me. Her face had a frown on it, and I could tell she felt helpless. "Do you need anything?"

"No, I think I'm good. I just want the pain to go away."

The phone rang, and she answered it on the first ring. She asked me more questions and listened patiently as the doctor gave her instructions. She hung up the phone and left my room. Returning, she handed me a glass of water, a pill and a heating pad.

"He suggested that you take a gas pill and use a heating pad. If the pain doesn't get better, we need to call him in the morning."

I did as she instructed and tried to go to sleep. But sleep didn't come easily. The pain was constant, and I started to worry as the hours ticked closer and closer to when I had to be ready and go to court. At some point, I finally dozed off.

My mom entered my room as my alarm clock started ringing. Hitting snooze, she looked at me. "How are you feeling?"

"A little bit better," I said as I sat up.

"Do you think you will be fine to go to court?"

"I think so."

She smiled at me and then gave me a hug before leaving the room. I went over to my closet and looked at the dress I would be wearing. It was black and came from one of my mom's huskier friends. It made me look like I was a bigger girl rather than a pregnant one. I sat on the bed waiting for the clock to tick away. It was only 7:15, and we didn't have to arrive until 8:30. Alone with my thoughts, I wondered how my life could go so wrong. How did I become obsessed with a guy who got me pregnant? We were so careful. And now, I was here; I was in the last stages of my pregnancy, giving a baby up for adoption, running from anyone who might be cruel and judgmental to me. And he was in jail. I wondered if he ever thought about me and if he cared that I was giving away our baby. I wondered what he would do when he heard my side of the story. We can't lie anymore. Everyone knew he was ten years older than I was, and in Georgia that was considered statutory rape. He would possibly get prison time. I pondered if I would ever see him again. Would he be gone for long? Next year I would be able to drive. Could I get away with sneaking up his way to see him? Would my parents ever trust me again, and would they allow me to drive anywhere except for an errand for them?

The time passed slowly as my thoughts meandered through my mind. I had the sudden urge to go to the bathroom, and as I stood up, I felt a gushing wetness between my legs. "Mom!" I yelled at the top of my lungs as I ran to the bathroom.

I was sitting on the toilet when my mom entered. "What is it, baby?"

"I just peed like a lot. Like I had to run to the bathroom."

Her face turned white, "Are you sure it was pee?"

"No..."

"Is it yellow?"

I got up from the toilet and looked. "No."

"Does it smell like pee?"

I looked at her with my nose scrunched up, puzzled at her question.

"If your mucus plug came out, it won't smell like urine."

I leaned my head close to the toilet. "It doesn't smell like pee."

My mom ran out of the room, and I sat back down. The fluid was still coming out in small, uncontrollable gushes. Returning, my mom had the phone to her ear while she handed me a diaper.

"What's the diaper for?" I asked my mom.

"That's to act as a pad soak up the fluids from your water breaking." She smiled. "I had to do it with you when my water broke."

My face went white with embarrassment.

"Yes, I'm calling about my daughter, Amanda. Her water just broke." My mom gestured for me to come out of the bathroom and sit in the dining room. "Okay, we are heading there shortly." She hung the phone up and immediately dialed the next person on the list: my dad. "Hey, James. Amanda's water broke, and we are heading to the hospital as soon as you get here."

I sat in my chair terrified to move a muscle. Even though I was in labor, I couldn't stop the fear of missing court. My impression was that you had to go to court, no matter what delayed you. Naïve to the court process, I was relieved to know that my stepdad could go in place of my mom, my dad and myself.

My mom placed my hospital bag next to my chair. While I was sitting there waiting for my dad, I called my close friends to let them know it was time. Moments before dad pulled up, my mom had me in the car and ready to go. I sat in the back seat so I could lie down if it made me feel more comfortable. I saw my dad's truck enter the driveway, and my mom began to back up. Daddy did not intend to exit his vehicle; he turned around and followed us out.

Racing down the highway, dad led the way flashing his lights and swerving like a madman. "Mom, why is he driving like that?"

"He's trying to get people out of our way so we can make it down to the hospital in time."

"Oh, ohhhh," I groaned as we took a sharp corner. My back was hurting worse than the night before.

"Are you alright?" my mom asked as she peered at me through the rearview mirror.

I nodded and closed my eyes. We finally pulled up to the hospital, but instead of walking in like last time, I was told to stay in the car. My mom ran in and grabbed a nurse. Within moments, they came through the doors with a wheelchair. After helping me to climb in the seat, the nurse wheeled me away.

In the labor and delivery room, I was hooked up to a monitor. My mom and dad joined me once they had the cars parked.

"Who's the father?" A nurse asked.

My dad was quick to respond, "I am." The nurse that asked the question and the others nurses in the room all turned to look at my dad. They began shooting daggers with their eyes. "No—no. Her father," he pointed to me. "I'm the baby's grandfather."

The angry looks died down, and the nurses went about their jobs to prepare for a new life to come into the world. One of the preparations was getting me ready for an epidural.

"She needs to be as still as possible. We are going to roll her over on her side. Dad," they were giving instructions to him, "you need to hold her like this." They had me on my side with my upper body curling toward my lower body.

I looked at my dad, "Why do I need to be still?"

"Because you could become paralyzed if they mess up."

I took a deep breath. The needle they were about to place in my back could possibly hurt me in ways I never imagined. "I feel sick," I said as my stomach continued to twist in agonizing knots.

My mom helped me get to the bathroom where I vomited water before I started dry heaving. As soon as I was done, the anesthesiologist was in the room ready for me to lie down so he could begin the process. My dad held me tightly as he could, to the point I was extremely uncomfortable. "Do you have to hold me so tight? It hurts."

"Only a little bit longer. Just be still." He was watching to make sure the entire process went as expected. My mom, on the other hand, was holding my hand and looking away. The thought of seeing the needle pierce my back made her nauseated.

I felt the prick and it was several minutes later that my dad finally released me. I was able to lie down on my back and wait for the next contraction. Before the next one could happen, my body began to feel less of a burden. I was still uncomfortable, but not like I was previously.

My dad held my hand, and every time a contraction hit, I squeezed, and then he squeezed back. "Daddy, can you not grip my hand so hard?"

I had to ask after every contraction.

"Oh," he would respond. "Sorry, baby."

While my dad was having little panic attacks at my side, my mom was interested in the monitor that was beside the bed. She looked at it with intense curiosity.

"Get away from there. You might set something off with your bag of stuff," My dad said. My mom always carried a huge purse, and it normally contained bags and bags of stuff. The only advantage of her bags was that she had everything at her disposal; the disadvantage was that it took her hours to go through and find anything.

As if on cue, the monitor started beeping. Startled, my mom rushed to the other side of the room. "Do you think I really set it off?"

"Why wouldn't you have?" My dad laughed.

A nurse ran in with several nurses behind him. He started barking orders at them. "Okay, we have to level her out and get her ready."

Ready? Was it happening already? Was I about to deliver? As if hearing my thoughts, my dad chimed in, "Level her? For what?"

The guy looked up at him and responded, "We are doing an emergency c-section."

"Why are they doing a c-section?" The creases on my dad's head deepened. "She is supposed to have the baby naturally."

"The doctor will be in here in a little bit to explain further, but right now we have to get her ready."

Waiting for what seemed like forever, the doctor finally stepped into the room. My mom asked before anyone else had a chance, "Why is she doing a c-section?"

"Because she is having placenta abruption; that's where the placenta separates from the uterine wall," the doctor said as if it was a common occurrence.

The doctor always seemed calm and very nonchalant, which was very different than how my family felt right then.

"How do you know? You weren't even in here." My mom asked.

"Because there is another patient delivering, and I'm able to monitor both patients," he smiled.

They increased my epidural dosage. I felt the coolness from the medicine release into my body. The nurse looked at me, "How do you feel?"

"Fine," I answered. The pain was gone, and I was feeling light-headed.

"I need you to do me a favor," he said. I nodded. "Lift your legs."

I felt confused. "I'm trying, but they aren't moving."

"Good. They don't need to. I'm just checking to make sure. Ok, now, squeeze my finger." He placed his finger in my hand. I wrapped my hand around it but was unable to grip it.

He smiled, "Good. She's ready to go," he told the staff in the room. "Who's going with her?" He asked as he looked at my mom and dad.

"Can we both not go?" My mom asked.

"No, we only allow one person to go."

"I'll go," my dad said, as my mom stepped into the hall.

Handing my dad his blue scrubs, they wheeled me to the operating room.

I was without my parents, wheeled away to be cut open. Would they make it there in time? I feared they wouldn't. I'd never had surgery. I watched the ceiling tiles pass above me as we turned a corner here and then turned another corner there. With no idea where I was going, I hoped my dad would be close behind. Finally, I was wheeled into a room. Placing my current bed next to another, they had to lift me from one bed to the next. Then they put a blue blanket over me, so I couldn't see what was going on. Every now and then, a nurse would look at me and ask if I was alright.

I was relieved when I heard familiar voices. It was my mom's that I heard first. Why was she in here? Daddy was supposed to be by my side. As if hearing my thoughts, he popped up behind my blue curtain. "Hey baby, how are you doing?"

"I'm good. I thought I heard Mom?"

She peeked behind the curtain, dressed in blue like my dad. "I'm here," she smiled.

"How? I thought only one of you?"

My mom smiled brightly. "I finally asked the right person, and they decided to let me in."

A nurse popped around the contraption blocking my view. "Move your arm for me."

I tried moving it, but it wouldn't budge. The only thing I was capable of moving was my head and my fingers. But even those movements were minimal.

"Alright," the nurse added. "You will feel pressure, pushing and pulling, but you shouldn't feel any pain."

I took a deep breath. It was time. I looked at my dad, who placed his head close to mine and made sure that he couldn't see beyond the drape. My mom, on the other hand, was watching everything they were doing. I felt the pressure the nurse informed me of; they were doing something, but I couldn't feel any pain. Watching mom, I was fascinated as to what she saw. She would glance at me for a moment, then turn back to watch what was happening on the other side. Looking at the curtain, I watched blood spots hit the drape and watched them fly over my head.

"What are they doing?" I asked my dad.

My dad peeked around the curtain and quickly drew back to our shelter. "They have your guts all piled on your stomach."

The mental image was disturbing to me, yet fascinating. "Really?"

"Yeah," and then he laughed. "I can't believe your mom is watching that. She couldn't even watch the epidural."

I listened to the buzz that filled the room. People moved constantly. Metal objects clinked here and there with barked orders. I would squeeze my dad's hand, even though it was barely a grip. Then I heard, "It's a girl."

I didn't hear her cry. Instead, I heard what sounded like someone hitting another person really hard. Then I heard it. Her cry filled my heart in a way I never imagined. I wanted to see her and comfort her in that moment, but I had to wait. Tears left my eyes. Looking at my mom and dad, I saw they were crying right along with me.

The nurse finally brought the baby around, and I saw the life that I had been carrying within me. She was beautiful. She was more beautiful than I could have ever imagined. They took her out of the room and I felt an overwhelming sadness.

After placing my guts back in their rightful places and stapling me back up, the doctor soon told me I was ready to roll into the recovery room right next to my baby, who was being cleaned up. The nurse had her facing away from me, and she was crying as the nurse dug a swab in her ear to clean out the gunk. She then flipped her over and we locked eyes for the first time. She stopped crying.

"Hey, baby girl," I whispered. I was in awe at this tiny bundle. The nurse flipped her again. Facing away from me, she began to cry once more. This phenomenon amazed me. Did she already know who I was? And then as the nurse completed her cleaning duties, my little bundle of joy was flipped toward me. She stopped crying.

The Challenging Decision

Due to an unplanned C-section, my hospital stay went from two days to four. That gave me extra days with a little one who would hopefully look for me once she turned 18. I held her as much as I could. I enjoyed feeding her, and then when I laid her in her bed, I watched her. I was so in love. I never imagined that I would have such love for anyone. Then I felt ashamed.

Daggers hit my heart when I thought back to seven months ago when I tried to abort her. I hated myself for even having those thoughts. I hated Don for having those thoughts. God had another plan, and for that, I was thankful. It dawned on me that not finding the abortion clinic was what God intended. My mistake was made right... I hoped.

The first night in the hospital, my dad volunteered to stay, and my mom went home. I kept my head turned toward my baby while I sent prayers up above. I was asking God to watch over us and that He would guide me in the decision that would follow in a couple of days. Deep down, I didn't want to say goodbye. I wanted her to come home with me. I knew she would be taken care of with her new parents, but I never imagined this overpowering love I would have for her.

My eyes finally closed, and I slept. I had an extreme calm feeling come over me. I was dreaming, I knew, but I was in the hospital bed, and I was awake in my dream. I looked directly above me and saw a glorious face looking down at me. The face, surrounded by a glow, filled every dark crevice in the room. She was in a white gown, and I knew I was looking at an angel. The glow that I saw in the room seemed to be radiating from her. Even though her robe was a blinding white, I couldn't turn my head away. She smiled at me, and I smiled back. She then nodded her head toward my daughter.

Glancing at my beautiful baby, not even a day old, I noticed there was a man standing over her. He was in the same white robe the angel wore. His hands were placed on both sides of her bed and he was looking down at her. Knowing that I was watching, he looked up at me. His hair flowed to his shoulders, and his face was more radiant than the angel's. If I thought the angel was beautiful, this man was breathtaking. He nodded and smiled. I knew this man, but I was confused. Why would he choose to visit my baby and me? His name continued to repeat itself in my own thoughts: Jesus. He was standing there in my hospital room, looking at the little girl He sent to me. In that moment, I knew whatever happened, it was His plan, and He was in control. If she went home with me or went home with the parents, everything would be the way it should.

I awoke to the room filled with the radiant light I had seen in my dream. I watched as it slowly faded away. I looked over at my precious bundle to see that she was still sleeping, but only for a minute. She began moving and fussing. I found a bottle, picked her up, and fed her.

The next day, I had visitors that I never imagined would show up. My two best friends made their way to see me. My grandparents, my aunts, and others who wanted to show their support came. My mentor even came to see me. She also made sure that I had taken plenty of pictures before I had to say goodbye to my little one.

The adoptive parents also came to visit. "Do you want the baby in the room while you meet them?" asked Cheryl, the lady from the adoption center.

"I don't know." I looked to my mom and dad for guidance.

"I would send the baby to the nursery while you meet with them," my mom suggested.

"I think that would be best," my dad agreed.

So, that's what we did. We let her go to the nursery, and then I met the soon-to-be parents.

There are couples that look like they were made for each other. They match each other so well that you can just tell they are together. I call them salt and pepper couples because they make me think of a matching set of shakers. When the new parents walked in, I immediately thought they were made for each other. They were both average heights with brown hair and they both had slightly round faces. They also had smiles that pulled me in and made me feel happy and relaxed.

"Hey. I'm Clark, and this is Jane," the new father said.

"Hey, I'm Amanda," I said, and then my parents introduced themselves.

"How are you feeling?" Jane asked me.

"I feel fine. They made me get up and walk today. That was a little bit difficult, but I made it down to the cafeteria." It wasn't the most comfortable walk in my life, but I was glad to leave the room.

"That's good. So the delivery went well?" Jane asked.

I shrugged. I assumed it all went well. "They had to do a C-section, but other than that, I thought it went pretty good."

"Why did they have to do a C-section?" Clark asked.

My mom chimed in and explained the facts that I had trouble understanding.

"So is there anything you want to know about us, Amanda?" Jane asked.

I thought about it for a moment, and then finally found what I truly wanted to know. "Will you send pictures, and can I send her gifts?"

"Of course you can," Clark answered.

"Yes, we will send pictures. We figured twice a year, but you can send as much as you want." Jane added.

That eased my fear of missing the years in between now and when she turned 18. "I was also told that I should put together a booklet that had my journal I've been keeping and my personal information. That way, when she's old enough, she can search for me, and I'll be easy to find."

"That sounds great." Jane smiled.

We sat and talked non-stop. They felt like family that came to visit. Anyone looking in would have never guessed we all just met. Jane and Clark filled us in on their home. They told me about the spacious outdoors that Lainey, that's what they named her, would have to play in. They also told me about her room and all the stuff they had for her. I even found out that they had a baby shower, which I thought was interesting. However, it made sense.

Finally, they asked, "Can we see her?" I didn't even realize that they had yet to see her.

"Sure," my dad said, and he led them to the nursery.

I felt relief and comfort that I had chosen the right home for Lainey to go to. But the relief still didn't help the knowledge that I only had one more full day with her. The pain stung deeply, and I wasn't sure how I was going to handle it.

Gone for a short fifteen minutes, Clark and Jane returned to the room to say goodbye. "Can we come see you tomorrow?"

"Of course," I said with a smile on my face. I did want to get to know them better. After all, they were the parents that would be taking care of my child. "Maybe tomorrow we can have Lainey in the room with us."

"Oh, that would be great," Jane beamed.

The next day the adoptive parents returned, and we kept Lainey in the room. She stayed next to me for a while.

"Can I hold her?" Clark asked.

I nodded and picked up the little bundle from her bed. She barely made a peep. I kissed her on her forehead and handed her to Clark. I had just settled back in the hospital bed when Lainey began to cry. I watched as he tried soothing her, but she continued. She just ate, so she wasn't hungry. She had her diaper changed, so that wasn't the problem. I watched as he rocked her and was telling the listening ears in the room that he had read how to comfort a baby. Yet, she still cried. I began to cringe. I wanted to go and comfort her; I wanted to help soothe her. Though, I knew, it wasn't my place to soothe her. In two days, the soothing would be left to this couple.

My eyes began to water. I wanted to cry right along with Lainey. Excusing myself, I went to the bathroom. There I let the tears flow as I doubled over, holding onto the sink. The pain that hit my body was not what I had expected. I was sure that I was going to be okay with Lainey and the adoptive parents in the room, but now, I knew different. I pulled myself together. I dried the tears from my eyes, but I couldn't do anything about the red face that always followed the water works.

Walking back into the room wasn't easy because Lainey was still crying. The parents decided that it was time for them to go because they could see that I was upset. They handed Lainey to me, and in a couple of heartbeats, she stopped crying.

"Thank you, so much, Amanda," Clark and Jane said. The words were not meant for this short time they got to see Lainey. They were for the gift of life that I was able to give them, a gift I didn't want to give. I wanted Lainey to come home with me. I wanted to soothe her. I wanted to be the one she called Mom. I wanted to be the one who saw her grow up.

That night was the last night in my room. My mom was staying with me, and we decided we needed a hearty dinner, so we ordered steak and potatoes from a local restaurant. I started crying after taking a couple of bites.

"What's wrong, baby?" my mom asked as she came and sat on my bed.

I shook my head. I couldn't talk. She stroked my hair and then picked up the phone. "Let's call your Grandma in California ." I knew Mom was talking about her step-mom. This grandmother had a voice that was soothing, and she always had the right words for any situation.

My mom talked to her first and cried for a bit as my grandma coached her through this tough time we all were going through. Finally, she handed me the phone.

"Hey, Grandma," I said as cheerily as possible.

"Hey, Amanda. How are you?" came the voice I only heard once a year or so. With her living in California, we talked very seldom, but she was always there when I needed her wisdom.

"Not good," I admitted.

"What's going on?" her calm voice asked.

"I want to keep her, Grandma. I don't want to give her up." I started crying again. She waited patiently for me to control my emotions. Finally, my crying slowed down. "I don't know if she is supposed to go with them." The earlier scene played in my head. How would they soothe her and make her feel safe?

"Can I pray for you?" she asked.

"Yes," I said.

"Dear Lord, wrap your arms around Amanda and Lainey. Let them find calm in the middle of the storm. And, Lord, let them know the right decision to make. Let them make your decision. In Jesus' precious name, Amen."

I cried as I handed the phone to my mom. I knew God had a plan, I just didn't know what it was. I wanted it to be Lainey leaving with us. I so badly wanted it, but I knew that my life would change and that Lainey might not have the best life possible.

The next morning, my mom nudged me. "Get up, honey. The lawyers are here."

I sat up, confused. I looked to where Lainey was and noticed that her bed was gone. "Where's Lainey?"

"They took her to the nursery so that you could sign the papers."

My heart sank deep into the pit of my empty stomach. A lump formed in my throat that prevented me from speaking, and tears began to fill in the corner of my eyes. I nodded and looked around the room. The only ones in the room were my mom and my dad.

"Are you ready?" My dad asked me.

I nodded, the only response I could give. My dad sat behind me and supported me because I was unable to hold myself up. My mom stood next to the bed, not sure what she should be doing. Then the lawyers entered. They were both tall and wearing three-piece business suits.

"Hey, Amanda," said one of the lawyers. "My name is William Brown, and this is my assistant, Wayne. Are you ready to sign the papers?"

I didn't move. I didn't even lift my eyes to get a good look at them. To me, they were the enemy.

"Will it help you to know that Don didn't even hesitate when he signed the papers?"

That caught my attention. "He didn't?" My sorrow at that moment became a heated anger.

"No. It took him only about thirty minutes to sign it all."

Making a mental note, I looked at the clock to see what time it was. It read 8 a.m. The assistant placed the documents on the portable food tray and rolled it over to me. Handing me a pen, he began to explain the papers that sat before me.

"This paper states that you give all rights away to the adoptive parents."

I gasped as my heart exploded. I slowly picked up the pen and brought it down to the signature line. My hand began to shake. I stared at the line until it became a blur.

After several minutes passed, I shook my head. "I can't." I continued to shake. "I can't," I began to sob, repeatedly.

"Can she sign this paper last?" I felt the words rumble out of my dad's chest.

"She can," William replied. He flipped the page and started describing the legalities that were held there. I heard only half of what he said.

My dad pointed to a line, "Sign there."

"What's that one?" I asked.

"It says that if something happens to both adoptive parents, then Lainey would be placed back in your care."

If I initialed at the spot my dad pointed to, and if something were to happen to both the adoptive parents, God would place her back in my arms. It would be up to God and what He desired. I scribbled my initials. I continued to listen for cues to the spots my dad told me I needed to sign. As for the lawyers, I only heard mumbles. It was my dad who I heard; he was my translator. As the stack became smaller, my sobs became more frequent. There were times when I had to place the pen down, let my tears take over, and then pick up where I had stopped. I looked at the clock. It was now 10:00. So far, it was taking two hours, and I had yet to be finished. I was shocked that Don could sign the papers so quickly. How? How could he? She was his blood. His flesh!

My dad's arms were around me, hugging me tightly. It was his strength that supported me. I noticed at the hospital that he had aged over the past nine months. His blonde hair was still blonde, but the wrinkles on his face intensified and tunneled deeper. I was grateful he was there. If he wasn't, I doubt I would have been able to function.

"Initial this one," my dad said.

"This one?" I choked and pointed to the blurred line that was before me.

"Yes," he said.

My mom sat on the couch that was by the window. Her face was red and swollen from crying as she watched her baby cry, pleading to take care of the child she bore four days prior. When I agreed to adoption all those months ago, I never imagined how hard it would be to give up a piece of me. She was my flesh, my blood, my baby.

I choked on a sob and let the waterworks start again. The stack of papers continued to shrink, and the first page would soon be on top again.

It was the page I didn't want to see. The page I didn't want to come.

Someone in the room made a remark that they had never dealt with so much emotion in an adoption case. How heartless could people be? I couldn't wrap my mind around it. I was only fifteen, and I had seen more miracles than I could ever imagine. The biggest miracle was my inability to believe that my blunder could make such a perfect little person.

That was the end of the papers. I only had one more to sign. The lawyers flipped the stack of papers back to the first page.

I stared through puffy, watery eyes. I didn't know how much time had passed, but I felt my dad nudge me. "You can do it," he said.

I choked and started sobbing again. People who heard me must have thought I was a hysterical mess.

My dad held me until my weeping started to subside.

I looked back at my last line to sign. Once again, I stared into oblivion and then I started shaking my head, "no, no, no, no, no. I can't." My teeth were gritted as I forced the words out. "I can't."

My dad released a sob, "Baby," he said, "you can."

From the many gifts that surrounded me, my dad grabbed an inspirational book and opened it. That's what we did when we needed direction. We trusted that the Lord would show us guidance through words, and all we had to do was open the Bible or an inspirational book with no destination in mind. The verse or words of wisdom would be all that we needed to lead us.

Knowing God would put us on the right path, my dad read the passage quietly to himself. He began to cry and placed the book in my hand to the page he had just read.

"'For God so loved the world that he gave his only begotten son, that whoever shall believeth shall not perish, but have everlasting life.' John 3:16."

I sobbed at the words before me and nodded my head with a new strength. I looked at my dad, "If God could give his only son, I can give my daughter."

I picked up the pen and signed my name to the line that stated I no longer had any rights over my child. My own flesh. My own blood.

I felt my soul rip from my body as I flew back into my dad's arms.

I screamed, cried, and was in complete delirium, sobbing, "My baby, my baby. I want my baby."

I was allowed five more minutes with Lainey. My dad and mom exchanged guard, and it was now my mom who held me up. "Amanda, you have to calm down. Lainey will be upset if you are upset."

I tried controlling my rapid breathing by taking deep breaths and then exhaling. At last, I calmed myself enough for them to bring Lainey to me. It was time for her to eat, so I was handed a bottle as well. Our eyes stayed locked on each other, and I continued to cry quietly as I fed her.

Cheryl stepped into the room. "Amanda," she said quietly.

I knew what her presence meant. I nodded to let her know, I knew. I couldn't speak. The vice was around my throat again, choking any noise that wanted to exit. I kissed Lainey on the head as Cheryl picked her up. My heart throbbed, and my stomach felt raw. The grip released, and I began to sob again. I rolled over on the bed and let the pain wash over me.

The Move Forward

I had ten days to change my mind after signing the papers. Following the adoption, I fell into a depression: I slept a ton and I barely ate. As the tenth day arrived, the lawyer called asking if my decision had changed. I hesitated for a moment before finally letting them know that she would have a better life with her adoptive parents.

Going back to school, I felt different. I finally felt like a normal teenager. Besides people questioning why I wasn't in school for almost two months, I was pretty much accepted back with open arms. Because of adoption, I was able to live a regular teenage life and I was able to graduate high school. Because of adoption, Lainey was able to live a life that a child should live. She has two parents that are able to provide for her. She has room to grow and won't have to worry about going without food or shelter. Adoption saved us both and granted the both of us a chance to live the best life possible. Beyond living our lives, adoption granted us a chance to live the life God has called us to live.

It's hard to believe this happened that long ago.

The adoption center was the go-between for contact between the adoptive parents and me. I wasn't allowed to have their address or last name to help protect them in case I was to try something crazy, such as kidnapping. I received photos up until she was about 11. I'm not sure if the adoptive parents stopped sending photos or not, but the non-profit organization changed hands and they stopped doing adoptions. My last trip to the center, I found out that the go-between should have been the lawyer and never the adoption center. My heart broke that day, but I am still in good hopes that one day I will get a chance to meet Lainey and hopefully build a lasting relationship with her.

As for Don, he only received nine months of boot camp and 18 years probation. I went to see him one afternoon after I received my drivers license. I wanted to tell him all about his daughter and fill him in on what had happened over a year ago with my side of the story.

He fed me lines as he did when I first met him, but I was a different person. I no longer fell for his smooth words. It was in that moment that I realized his love was no match for the love I had for our daughter. His love was for something I no longer wanted him to have. Leaving his driveway, I didn't look back.

I had a future. God would use me. I didn't know then how or why, but I knew He would take my mistake and make it my defining moment.

Acknowledgments

Writing a book isn't easy. Writing a personal story such as this is demanding. I relived many moments that drained me emotionally. Thank you to the family and friends who listened to my constant babble as I tried to work out my emotions. Your support is everything to me.

To my editors, you are lifesavers. It was your hard work and belief in me that helped me along in this journey. I'm sorry for all the crazy comma use, irrational tenses, and vague descriptions. From the bottom of my heart, I thank you all for your help and support.

About the author

I'm a wife, a mom, a student of life, a daughter, a sister, a friend, an author, a journalist, and most definitely a dreamer ...

I'm always dreaming and writing.

Made in the USA
Columbia, SC
09 May 2024

35495624R00052